WEATHER AROUND YOU
RAIN

Anita Ganeri

EARLY LEARNING LIBRARY

Please visit our web site at: www.earlyliteracy.cc
For a free color catalog describing Weekly Reader® Early Learning Library's list
of high-quality books, call 1-877-445-5824 (USA) or 1-800-387-3178 (Canada).
Weekly Reader® Early Learning Library's fax: (414) 336-0164.

Library of Congress Cataloging-in-Publication Data

Ganeri, Anita, 1961-
  Rain / Anita Ganeri.
    p. cm. — (Weather around you)
  Includes index.
  ISBN 0-8368-4299-5 (lib. bdg.)
  ISBN 0-8368-4304-5 (softcover)
  1. Rain and rainfall—Juvenile literature. 2. Floods—Juvenille literature.
  I. Title.
  QC924.7.G36   2004
  551.57'7—dc22   2004041891

This North American edition first published in 2005 by
Weekly Reader® Early Learning Library
330 West Olive Street, Suite 100
Milwaukee, WI 53212 USA

This U.S. edition copyright © 2005 by Weekly Reader® Early Learning Library. Original edition
copyright © 2004 by Hodder Wayland. First published in 2004 by Hodder Wayland, an imprint of
Hodder Children's Books, a division of Hodder Headline Limited, 338 Euston Road, London NW1 3BH, UK.

Commissioning Editor: Vicky Brooker
Book Editor: Katie Sergeant
Book Designer: Jane Hawkins
Picture Researcher: Katie Sergeant

Weekly Reader® Early Learning Library Art Direction: Tammy West
Weekly Reader® Early Learning Library Cover Design and Page Layout: Kami M. Koenig
Weekly Reader® Early Learning Library Editor: Barbara Kiely Miller

Photo Credits
The publisher would like to thank the following for permission to reproduce their photographs:
Alamy: Contents page (Royalty-free), 8 (Goodshoot); Corbis: 6 (Ken Straiton), 7 (Jose Luis Pelaez, Inc.), 9 (Craig Tuttle),
12 (Joe McDonald), 16 (Marc Rebuttini), 17 (Philip Wallick), 18 (Doug Miner), 19 (Bettmann), 20 (James A. Sugar),
22, 23, 24 (Micheal Keller); Corbis/Ecoscene: 13 (Chinch Gryniewicz); Getty: Cover (Photodisc Red/Royalty-Free),
4 (The Image Bank/Yellow Dog Productions), 15 (Taxi/Gail Shumway); OSF: 5 (David Cayless), 14 (Dinodia Picture Agency);
Science Photo Library: 10 (David Nunuk), 11 and Title page (Adam Hart-Davis), 21 (Rev. Ronald Royer).

Printed in China

1 2 3 4 5 6 7 8 9 08 07 06 05 04

Contents

Words in **bold** can be found in the glossary on page 23.

A Rainy Day

What do you like to do on a rainy day?
Do you like to go outside and splash in
the puddles?

Playing in the rain can be fun. We also need rain for water. But too much rain can make life hard for people and animals.

What Is Rain?

Rain is made up of drops of water. These drops are called raindrops. They are shaped like bubbles with flat bottoms. You can see them splashing on the window.

Raindrops can be big or small. Sometimes small drops fall, and the rain is light. Light rain is called **drizzle**. The raindrops in a heavy **shower** are as big as peas.

How Does Rain Fall?

The Sun shines on the oceans, lakes, and rivers. The Sun heats up the water. Some of this warm water turns into **water vapor**. It rises up into the air.

As the water vapor rises, it cools down. Some of it turns into tiny drops of water. Millions of drops make a rain cloud. The wind blows rain clouds across the sky.

Inside a rain cloud, the drops of water bump into each other. Many drops join together to make bigger and bigger drops.

Soon the drops are too big and heavy to stay up in the air. They fall from the cloud to the ground as rain.

Water for Life

Animals and plants need water to stay alive. Farmers use rain to water their **crops**. If the crops die, people and animals do not have enough to eat.

People need water for drinking, cooking, and washing. Some rainwater is collected in large lakes called **reservoirs**. Some is pumped up from underground by wells.

Heavy Rains

Some countries have months of heavy rain each year. In India, the rain lasts from June to September. This season of rain and wind is called a **monsoon**.

Rain forests grow around the **equator**. They are warm and wet all year. The rain helps plants grow. Millions of animals live among the rain forest plants.

Flood Warning!

Sometimes a lot of heavy rain falls in a short time. So much rain can make rivers overflow. Water that spills over its **banks** onto land is called a **flood**.

Floods can be harmful. Too much water soaks farmers' fields and spoils the crops. Floods can wash away bridges and roads and ruin buildings.

Living with Floods

People put **sandbags** around their houses to keep the water out. They move their furniture upstairs. If the flood is very bad, they have to leave their homes.

In a flood, the water covers the roads.
Cars and buses cannot get through.
People can only get around by boat or air.

Too Little Rain

Sometimes people expect rain, but it does not come. A long time of dry weather is called a **drought**. The land, rivers, and lakes dry up. Plants die. People and animals do not have enough to eat or drink.

The desert is dry for most of the year. Many plants cannot grow there. But seeds of some plants lie hidden underground. After a shower of rain, the seeds burst into flower.

Rain Fact File

- The rainiest place in the world is Mount Waialeale in Hawaii. It rains there about 335 days every year.

- Arica in Chile has the lowest amount of rainfall in the world. It only gets a trickle of rain each year. Another place in Chile, called Calama, had no rain at all for four hundred years from 1570 to 1971.

- Sometimes, instead of rain, hail falls from rain clouds. Hail is made up of tiny crystals of ice. The biggest hailstone that ever fell was as big as a melon!

- When the Sun comes out after a rain shower, you might see a colorful rainbow. A rainbow is made when the Sun shines through raindrops. The colors in a rainbow are red, orange, yellow, green, blue, indigo, and violet.

Glossary

banks — the land at the edge of a river or lake

crops — plants that farmers grow for food

drizzle — very light rain with small raindrops

drought — a time when the land is very dry

equator — an imaginary line around the middle of Earth

flood — rising water that covers the land after a lot of heavy rain

monsoon — a long time of very heavy rainfalls in countries such as India

reservoirs — large lakes, built by people, that fill up with rainwater for drinking and watering crops

sandbags — sacks that are filled with sand

shower — a brief rainfall

water vapor — water that has turned into an invisible gas

Index

About the Author

Anita Ganeri is an award-winning author of children's information books. She has written many books about geography and the natural world.